ADVENT
Season of Divine Encounter

Amy Ekeh

*A ministry of the Diocese of Little Rock
in partnership with Liturgical Press*

Nihil obstat: Jerome Kodell, OSB, *Censor Librorum.*
Imprimatur: ✠ Anthony B. Taylor, Bishop of Little Rock, February 2, 2018.

Cover design by Ann Blattner. Cover photo: Getty Images. Used with permission.

Photos/illustrations: Pages 7, 11, 13, 14, 15, 20, 23, 24, 27, 31, 33, 35, 36, 38, Getty Images. Used with permission. Page 26, Liturgical Press Archives.

ISBN: 978-0-8146-4462-1 (print); 978-0-8146-4485-0 (ebook)

Contents

Introduction

Alive in the Word brings you resources to deepen your understanding of Scripture, offer meaning for your life today, and help you to pray and act in response to God's word.

Use any volume of **Alive in the Word** in the way best suited to you.

- **For individual learning and reflection,** consider this an invitation to prayerfully journal in response to the questions you find along the way. And be prepared to move from head to heart and then to action.

- **For group learning and reflection,** arrange for three sessions where you will use the material provided as the basis for faith sharing and prayer. You may ask group members to read each chapter in advance and come prepared with questions answered. In this kind of session, plan to be together for about an hour. Or, if your group prefers, read and respond to the questions together without advance preparation. With this approach, it's helpful to plan on spending more time for each group session in order to adequately work through each of the chapters.

- **For a parish-wide event or use within a larger group,** provide each person with a copy of this volume, and allow time during the event for quiet reading, group discussion and prayer, and then a final commitment by each person to some simple action in response to what he or she learned.

This volume on the topic of Advent is one of several volumes that explore **Liturgical Seasons**. Our church accents seasons within each year in which to enter into the story of salvation. This is commonly referred to as the liturgical calendar. Its purpose is not to mark the passage of time but to understand the overall mystery of salvation in Jesus Christ, from his incarnation and birth through his ministry, death, resurrection, and sending of the Spirit. By meditating on the themes of these various seasons in the church year, we are more fully able to live the mystery of Christ in our own lives.

Prologue

[Handwritten notes in margins:]

"Advent" means "coming"

advent season reflecting on how we can prepare our hearts and home for Christ's birth in the world as it is today

It's a sign of hope and it fills me with peace

Our yearly celebration of the season of Advent is a time of both recollection and anticipation. The word "advent" comes from the Latin verb *advenire*, which means "to arrive" or "to come to." Of course, during Advent, we focus on the arrival of Jesus. We recall his birth, his "becoming flesh," his coming into our world. We also look forward to his return in faithful expectation of that time when, in the words of St. Paul, God will be "all in all" (1 Cor 15:28).

But as we remember the past and anticipate the future, we must not forget the present. The birth of Jesus has ushered in a new era, a time in which *God is present* with his people in a new and intimate way. This divine presence is a daily reality, and our ability to recognize the ways God "arrives" in our everyday lives has the power to change our hearts and change our world. In fact, this ongoing divine-human encounter is the central message of Scripture and the definitive experience of our lives.

To help us enter into the sacredness of this season of divine presence—as a *past, present, and future* reality—we will reflect together on passages from Scripture that help us recall, recognize, and anticipate encounters with God in our lives. How does God encounter his people? How does God encounter you?

6

[Handwritten notes at bottom:]

the circular wreath has no beginning and no end. Just like God's love for us and his never...

Tidbit: advent wreath is often described as a symbol of eternal life

Encountering God

in the Incarnate Word

Begin by asking God to assist you in your prayer and study. Then read John 1:14-18, a portion of the prologue of the Gospel of John.

John 1:14-18

[14]And the Word became flesh
and made his dwelling among us,
and we saw his glory,
the glory as of the Father's only Son,
full of grace and truth.

[15]John testified to him and cried out, saying, "This was he of whom I said, 'The one who is coming after me ranks ahead of me because he existed before me.'" [16]From his fullness we have all received, grace in place of grace, [17]because while the law was given through Moses, grace and truth came through Jesus Christ. [18]No one has ever seen God. The only Son, God, who is at the Father's side, has revealed him.

Handwritten annotations:

Jesus went thru the whole cycle of a human life — shows Christians that God understands their needs

The Unity of divinity w/ humanity in Jesus Christ

The incarnate shows us that God fully loves us. enough to make a way for us. thru Jesus

Jesus' Ministry is Marked both by Truth and grace

the gift of the incarnation all of life is Gods gracious gift

After a few moments of quiet reflection on John 1:14-18, consider the background information found in "Setting the Scene." Occasional questions in this section and the following may be used for personal reflection, journaling, or group discussion.

Setting the Scene

Advent presents us with a spiritual challenge. On one hand, nothing could be more natural than anticipating the birth of Jesus. But on the other hand, how do we anticipate something that has already taken place? To answer this, we can rely on the rich legacy of Judaism in *remembering* and *making present*.

In the Old Testament, we find countless examples of the Jewish people recalling and extolling the great acts of God, the ways God "got involved" with human beings. Two premier examples of these great acts are creation and the Israelites' exodus (departure) from Egypt. In the book of Genesis, creation is described as an act of power and generosity, with human beings as the apex of creation, made to be in relationship with God. In the book of Exodus, the Israelite people are liberated from slavery in a spectacular manner, protected as a journeying community, and eventually enter a land promised to them by God.

Throughout the Old Testament, as these works of God are recalled and told again and again (see Psalm 77 for an excellent example), it is as though these events and God's powerful presence in them are realized afresh. They become *present realities*. The God who "fixed the earth on its foundation" (Ps 104:5) and "did wonders, in the land of Egypt" (Ps 78:12) is present *here and now* in the very remembering. In effect, the mighty deeds of the past tell us not so much *who God was in the past* as *who God is in the present*. He is powerful and generous. He is in relationship with us. He liberates and protects.

This spiritual ability to recall and make present is important for us as we embark on our Advent journey. Of course, in a subsequent chapter we will consider how Advent challenges us to *look forward* with hope to the "end of the age," the time when Jesus will return as he promised. But for now, as we *look back* at the birth of Jesus, let us attempt to remember in an active and dynamic way that moves us past sentimental recollection and into a real divine encounter.

One thing that will help us in this spiritual challenge is to reflect on the birth of Jesus not only as an event in history but as a central mystery of our faith that we call *incarnation*. As we know, incarnation refers to the extraordinary act of God becoming human (*incarnare* is a Latin word meaning "to become flesh"). During Advent, we reflect deeply on this great mystery of our faith. It is a mystery that reaches far deeper and wider than the image of a baby in a manger (though there is great spiritual depth in that image alone!) Incarnation is a profound recognition of God's presence in our world in such a way that it has touched every human being deeply, profoundly, and intimately. Indeed,

Imitate the Israelites by recalling some of God's "mighty deeds" in your own past. How does this recollection help you to recognize God's presence in your past? What does it tell you about God? How does *remembering* help you understand the present and the future differently?

Physical reminder of God (a way to hold on to what they knew to be true even when doubt tried to tell them otherwise)

Incarnation — God Becoming Human

memories can help us to see and Remember God at work

the Vatican II fathers wrote that "by his incarnation, he, the Son of God, has in a certain way united himself with each individual" (*Gaudium et Spes* 22).

As we look together at a short passage from the prologue of John's gospel, we will simultaneously recall, make present, and anticipate the incarnation of Jesus. This may sound complicated or like a great spiritual feat. But as we unpack this rich passage, we will find that God's word has the power to open our minds and hearts to the dynamic reality of divine presence—*God makes his dwelling among us!*

John's prologue (1:1-18), from which we will read a brief excerpt, is widely regarded as one of the most densely packed, highly christological, elegantly beautiful passages in the New Testament. It is a spiritual masterpiece with a central theme: the Incarnate Word of God, Jesus Christ, has come into the world to reveal God to human beings. As we consider the final five verses of John's prologue, we will return to these themes of incarnation and revelation several times.

Themes

The passage from John 1:14-18 will be considered a few verses at a time in the section below.

Understanding the Scene Itself

[14]**And the Word became flesh
and made his dwelling among us,
and we saw his glory,
the glory as of the Father's only Son,
full of grace and truth.**

If remembering God's mighty deeds makes them present to us, then for Christians, one of the central deeds to remember is the incarnation of God in our world. In this verse from John's prologue, John explicitly recalls this great, humble act of God: taking on flesh, becoming human, accepting all that being human means, and simultaneously showing us his glory.

This verse tells us several important things about the one who is called "the Word." We might first ask ourselves: *What is a word? What is its purpose?* A word exists to communicate, to reveal, to tell something. A word exists to share meaning. We will return to this idea of *telling* and *revealing*.

In addition to considering the basic meaning of "word," it is useful to know both the Greek and Jewish backgrounds of this key term because both influences are likely at work here. The earliest readers of John's gospel would have recognized the term *logos* (Greek for "word") as a Greek philosophical concept that described the mind of the divine—its logic, order, and power—which was communicated to the world and human beings. The order of the cosmos and the rationality of the human mind, for example, derived from this divine *logos*. While this Greek usage may not be the primary influence in John's prologue, it certainly is not in conflict with it, and its meaning may have enhanced early interpretations of this passage. Certainly the Word in John's gospel has given order to the world (John 1:3) and is the agent through which human beings come to know the divine mind (1:18).

The Hebrew background of "word" (the Hebrew word *dabar* is used in the Old Testament) takes us even deeper into understanding John's depiction of Jesus as "the Word." In the Old Testament, the Hebrew Scriptures, God's word has great power and purpose. God creates simply by speaking words (e.g., Gen 1:3), his prophets carry on centuries of fearless ministry by speaking God's word on his behalf (e.g., Jer 1:9), and God's word is even personified as a potent, active presence that is sent into the world to accomplish God's will: "So shall my word be that goes forth from my mouth; it shall not return to me empty, but shall do what pleases me, achieving the end for which I sent it" (Isa 55:11).

In Jewish interpretation, God's *word* was also closely associated with God's *wisdom*. It seems clear that as he wrote his prologue, John was intentionally hearkening back to the following passage from the book of Sirach (composed second century BC). Here God's wisdom is associated with the covenant law of Israel. The law was holy, as though God was *dwelling within it*, because it was the way of life, love, and worship that bound Israel so closely to her God. In Sirach 24, we read this fascinating personification of God's wisdom:

> In a prayer spoken near the end of his life, Jesus said to the Father, "Your word is truth." Jesus is God's Word. How is Jesus the central truth of your life? How does his presence with you ground your life and give it purpose?

[handwritten note: Jesus, help us change our lives, face our trials & more. Us forward w/ Faith as we journey toward him/God]

³"From the mouth of the Most High I [Wisdom] came forth, and covered the earth like a mist. . . .

⁶Over waves of the sea, over all the land,
  over every people and nation I held sway.

⁷ Among all these I sought a resting place.
  In whose inheritance should I abide?

⁸Then the Creator of all gave me his command,
  and my Creator chose the spot for my tent.
He said, 'In Jacob make your dwelling,
  in Israel your inheritance.'

⁹Before all ages, from the beginning, he created me,
  and through all ages I shall not cease to be. . . .

¹²I struck root among the glorious people,
  in the portion of the Lord, his heritage."
  (Sir 24:3, 6-9, 12)

Another spectacular Old Testament passage, Proverbs 8:22-31, also depicts Wisdom as pre-existing with God, assisting God at creation as an "architect" or "artisan," and dwelling with human beings. In John's prologue, we hear clear echoes of passages such as these from the Hebrew Scriptures. Note, for example, John's declaration that the Word "made his dwelling among us." This phrase literally means that the Word "tabernacled" or "pitched his tent" among

How does the description of Wisdom from the book of Sirach correspond with the incarnation of the Word? Can you hear echoes of the life of Christ in this ancient text that predates his birth?

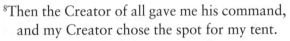

Encountering God in the Incarnate Word 13

he within the covenant
be faithful to God even in the
small thing

us, just like Wisdom in Sirach 24:8: "my Creator chose the spot for my tent." That "spot" is with God's "glorious people." That "spot" is "among us."

A final note on John's use of "Word" in this passage: Words are not typically spoken in a vacuum. Words are spoken between persons. Words are part of a relationship. The one who hears the word of another must respond to it—either by ignoring it, resisting it, accepting it, or embracing it. Later in the gospel, Jesus will make clear that he hopes we will listen to and believe in his word and that his word (meaning he himself) will dwell within us (John 5:24, 15:7).

Let us briefly consider several more important phrases from this jam-packed verse. Of course, the major "action" of the Word in this verse is *becoming flesh.* This bold statement leaves no room for debate whether or not this *Logos* who "was God" and who "was with God" (see John 1:1) has become a human being. John also writes that "we saw his glory." This statement of witness ("we saw") is a common theme of Johannine writings (see, for example, 1 John 1:1-3). The Word is now present among us, to be seen and touched, revealing to us something beyond this world: the glory (*doxa*) of God.

Recall a time in your life when words deeply impacted and enriched a relationship. How does Jesus as God's Word deeply impact and enrich your relationship with God? What has God said to you in Jesus?

Finally, we learn something very important about the relationship between the Word and God: it is the relationship of a Father and his "only Son." This characteristically Johannine language of "Father and Son" will be crucial in the early church's understanding of God as relationship, a relationship we all have access to now that the Word has become flesh.

[15]John testified to him and cried out, saying, "This was he of whom I said, 'The one who is coming after me ranks ahead of me because he existed before me.'"

John's prologue is interspersed with several "interruptions" about John the Baptist, and this single verse is one of them. This tongue-twisting and mind-bending declaration by the Baptist not only insists upon Jesus' superiority ("ranks ahead of me") but also proclaims the preexistence of the Word ("existed before me"). John the Baptist's words reaffirm the claim made by John the Evangelist in the first verse of his gospel ("In the beginning . . . the Word was with God"). This preexistence, associated with divinity, will later be explicitly claimed by Jesus himself (John 8:58). Again we are reminded that the now-incarnate-Word existed before anything was created. Awe-inspiring!

Every Advent, the Lectionary readings invite us to recall the ministry and testimony of John the Baptist. John said that he came to "make straight the way of the Lord" (John 1:23; see Isa 40:3). How can we imitate John the Baptist by being voices in the wilderness that "make straight the way of the Lord" in our world?

¹⁶From his fullness we have all received, grace in place of grace, ¹⁷because while the law was given through Moses, grace and truth came through Jesus Christ.

As our passage continues, John writes of the grace we have received through the incarnation of the Word, who is now identified by name and title: Jesus Christ. The title *Christ* is the Greek rendering of the Hebrew word "messiah," which means "anointed."

From Jesus Christ, the incarnate Son of the Father, we have all received grace. While some translations of this passage prefer "grace *upon* grace" (which would mean more and more grace), the NABRE prefers "grace *in place of* grace." This latter translation makes sense given the verse immediately following: "because while the law was given through Moses, grace and truth came through Jesus Christ." If we consider the basic meaning of the word "grace" as gift, we can understand what John is telling us. The law (given through Moses) was pure gift. It was God's gift of himself to his people—a pledge of faithfulness, a way of life, an encouragement toward covenant love and worship of the one true God. According to John, we now have an *even greater gift* in the person of Jesus Christ. God has not only communicated himself through the covenant but through his own Son.

> John associates Jesus with the word "grace" (1:14, 16). Grace means gift. Jesus is a generous, voluntary, unexpected, and undeserved gift. How has this gift arrived (*advenire*) in your life? In what areas of your life do you most experience this grace?

¹⁸No one has ever seen God. The only Son, God, who is at the Father's side, has revealed him.

John's gorgeous prologue comes to an end with these profound words. First John insists that no one has ever seen God. Even Moses, who spoke with God "face to face, as a person speaks to a friend" (Exod 33:11), did not see God as God really is. But those who have read John's entire prologue know that the Word has been with God from the beginning and that the Word is God (John 1:1). Only the Word, who has been identified as the Son of the Father and as Jesus Christ, has truly seen God in all of his glory, from a time before time existed.

In the verse above, John describes Jesus by saying he is the "only Son" and "God." A vivid phrase then declares that the Son "is at the Father's side." Other translations read "is close to the Father's heart" (NRSV), "is turned toward the Father" (Francis J. Moloney, *The Gospel of John*, Sacra Pagina series), or "is in the bosom of the Father" (KJV).

Finally, John sets forth a major theme of his gospel and indeed of Christian faith: "The only Son . . . has revealed him [the Father]." This Word, which speaks, tells, and communicates, has a single purpose: to reveal the Father. As we know, the Son will ultimately reveal the Father on the cross as a God of boundless, self-giving love. Incarnation, crucifixion, and redemption are one grand divine-human moment in salvation history, a moment inaugurated by the birth of Jesus, a moment we recall, encounter, and anticipate in our Advent longing.

In what ways does Jesus reveal the Father to you? How can you renew your sense of encounter with the Father this Advent?

Praying the Word / Sacred Reading

Ponder for several moments the awesome reality of God incarnate. As the book of Revelation declares: "God's dwelling is with the human race" (21:3).

Now slowly pray the following (a eucharistic preface prayed by the church during Advent). As you say it, take time to ponder each line:

> For all the oracles of the prophets foretold
>   him,
> the Virgin Mother longed for him
> with love beyond all telling,
> John the Baptist sang of his coming
> and proclaimed his presence when he came.
>
> It is by his gift that already we rejoice
> at the mystery of his Nativity,
> so that he may find us watchful in prayer
> and exultant in his praise.
>   (Eucharistic Preface II of Advent)

Living the Word

In a commentary on John's gospel (Sacra Pagina series, Liturgical Press), biblical scholar Francis Moloney paraphrases the final verse of John's prologue (1:19) with the profound conclusion: "He [Jesus] has told God's story."

As disciples of Jesus, we strive to imitate him. How can we tell God's story in our families and communities this Advent? Some ideas are below.

Choose one, or an idea of your own, and put it into action during this season of divine encounter.

- <u>*Renew your commitment to pray with your*</u> └
  <u>*family,*</u> *sharing with them your love of God.*

- *Join a social outreach ministry in your parish community, telling God's story of love* <u>*by helping others.*</u> *Angel tree*

- *Take up a cause of social justice that you have felt like giving up on in the past. It is easy to become discouraged, but God's story is not one of defeat and apathy. It is a story of presence and hope!* *Rosary*

- *If you feel so called, ask at your parish about becoming a catechist either in a youth or adult setting. Is God calling you to share his story by witnessing in this way?*

- *Invite a friend or loved one whom you have not seen in a while into your home. Make a date and keep it. We tell God's story best by being with each other.*

- *Visit an elder from your parish or town community. Let this person tell you God's story in his or her own way, either in words or simply by being. Share in the divine wisdom so often present in a long life.*

Recognizing Our Daily Divine Encounters

After spending a few moments inviting Go[d]
to accompany you, prayerfully read throug[h]
the first ten verses of Psalm 139, a prayer [of]
divine encounter.

Psalm 139:1-10

¹Lᴏʀᴅ, you have probed me, you know me:
  ²you know when I sit and stand;
  you understand my thoughts from afar.
³You sift through my travels and my rest;
  with all my ways you are familiar.
⁴Even before a word is on my tongue,
  Lᴏʀᴅ, you know it all.
⁵Behind and before you encircle me
  and rest your hand upon me.

⁶Such knowledge is too wonderful for me,
  far too lofty for me to reach.
⁷Where can I go from your spirit?
  From your presence, where can I flee?
⁸If I ascend to the heavens, you are there;
  if I lie down in Sheol, there you are.
⁹If I take the wings of dawn
  and dwell beyond the sea,
¹⁰Even there your hand guides me,
  your right hand holds me fast.

> *The background information in "Setting the Scene" will help you put the psalm in context within the Bible and within the season of Advent.*

Setting the Scene

In our last reflection, we contemplated the incarnation of the Word, a mystery of our faith that came about in the birth of Jesus. In reflecting on this past event, we considered how God is still present, "dwelling among us."

Our current passage, an excerpt from Psalm 139, will help us further contemplate God's ongoing presence with us. As we know *advent* means "to come to" or "to arrive." The psalmist reflects upon God's "arrival" in his life, inviting us to do the same.

The book of Psalms consists of 150 prayer-poems. Many, if not all, of these psalms were used in ancient liturgies and were probably sung. The psalms express a variety of human emotions—joy, fear, thanksgiving, sorrow, praise, confusion, even the desire for revenge! But in the

[Handwritten margin note: The Psalms express a variety of emotions]

midst of their variety, the psalms have in common a penetrating honesty and an unshakable trust in the God to whom they are addressed.

The psalms help us understand how the ancient Israelites prayed, allowing us to learn from this rich legacy. As we reflect more on the excerpt of Psalm 139 below, these words can become our own prayer as we thoughtfully place them in the context of the Advent season. As the psalmist recognizes God's intimate presence in his life, we can become more aware of God's presence with us and the boundless ways God "arrives" in our lives.

You now have the opportunity to explore in more detail the verses of Psalm 139. Use the questions in the margin for your own personal prayer and reflection or as the basis of discussion with others.

Understanding the Scene Itself

¹Lord, you have probed me, you know me:
  ²you know when I sit and stand;
  you understand my thoughts from afar.
³You sift through my travels and my rest;
  with all my ways you are familiar.
⁴Even before a word is on my tongue,
  Lord, you know it all.

As our psalm begins, the psalmist poetically asserts the omniscience—or the all-knowing power—of God. A simple glance at the subjects and verbs in these four verses reflects the psalmist's firm belief in God's knowledge:

- *you have probed, you know (v. 1);*
- *you know, you understand (v. 2);*
- *you sift, you are familiar (v. 3);*
- *you know (v. 4).*

[handwritten margin note: GOD knows us when we rise in the morning He knows us when we go about our day he knows us when we lie down at night]

The repetition of similar phrases is intentional. God knows what God has created.

Significantly, the psalmist is not talking about God's knowledge of the universe or of that which is too complex for human beings. Rather, the psalmist is in awe of God's knowledge of *him!* What has God probed and known and understood? The psalmist! A glance at the objects of the sentences easily reveals this touching truth. The psalmist is saying that God understands:

- *me, me (v. 1);*
- *when I sit and stand, my thoughts (v. 2);*
- *my travels and my rest, all my ways (v. 3);*
- *it all (v. 4).*

[handwritten note: There is no place to hide from his presence.]

This is not just knowledge; this is *intimate* knowledge!

Note especially the language of *probing* and *sifting*. The psalmist wants us to know that God does not know us in a static way, as though he creates us, takes one look at us, and knows us once and for all. Rather, God is *actively knowing* us. This is a dynamic relationship, one in which God is constantly searching our

Verses 1-3 of this psalm utilize a variety of verbs and images to help us imagine God's intimate knowledge of us. Which word or phrase from these verses resonates with you? Why?

[handwritten note: God's knowledge of all things does not limit his intimate knowledge of us.]

Even though we know God is our creator who knows our hearts and our thoughts, we are still sometimes tempted to hide ourselves or our thoughts from God. How can this Advent be a time of honesty before the Lord as we encounter God anew? Can this psalm offer encouragement?

hearts, sifting our intentions, probing us in order to know us. This probing and sifting allows God to know us so well that he knows us in the past, present, and even the future: "even before a word is on my tongue."

[handwritten: Past Present Future]

⁵Behind and before you encircle me
   and rest your hand upon me.
⁶Such knowledge is too wonderful for me,
   far too lofty for me to reach.

The psalmist now adds a new layer to his prayer. Not only does God *know* the psalmist, but God *is with* the psalmist. Using anthropomorphic imagery (ascribing human attributes to the divine), the psalmist helps us envision God's presence. God is encircling him, and God's hand rests upon him. Here we have a wonderful image of God's presence: an encircling arm, the tender touch of a hand.

Next we get a sense of the psalmist's wonder at these realities. Remember, the psalmist was a traditional Israelite, one who believed in the utter transcendence of God. Israel esteemed her God as totally "other"— sacred, holy, set apart. God was so powerful that he created simply by speaking a word. He could part raging waters, crush enemies, flood or redeem the earth. This is the same God who

[handwritten margin note: when we are honest we build strength of character that will allow us to be of great service to God and to others]

knows when the psalmist sits and stands! This is the God who knows when *we* sit and stand. Israel's powerful God is intimately aware of our thoughts, words, and actions. Israel's transcendent God encircles us with his arm and rests his hand upon us.

It is no wonder the psalmist concludes, "Such knowledge is too wonderful for me!"

⁷Where can I go from your spirit?
    From your presence, where can I flee?
⁸If I ascend to the heavens, you are there;
    if I lie down in Sheol, there you are.
⁹If I take the wings of dawn
    and dwell beyond the sea,
¹⁰Even there your hand guides me,
    your right hand holds me fast.

The psalm now moves from praising God's *omniscience* to recognizing God's *omnipresence*. God is all-present; he is everywhere! But above all, he is with us.

The psalmist uses several literary devices to express this faith in God's uninterrupted presence. First he asks God two rhetorical questions: "Where can I go from your spirit? From your presence, where can I flee?" A note about God's spirit—this is not a reference to the Holy Spirit, the Third Person of the Trinity, as we understand God from a Christian point of view. Rather, in this Israelite prayer, God's spirit is a way of speaking about God's life, his dynamic presence, that which animates God and all the things God has created. The psalmist is asking if there is

> The psalmist is describing God to God. Of course, God already knows these things and does not need our affirmations or praise. So why do we pray in this way? How can speaking to God *about* God help your relationship with God?

Handwritten margin notes:
Prayer helps Build a relationship w/ God — Thanking Praising confessions asking for help

anywhere he can go to "flee" or "go from" this spirit. Now of course this does not mean that the psalmist really wishes to escape God's presence. This is simply a rhetorical device that has the effect of saying: "I doubt I could get away from you, God, even if I wanted to!"

Indeed, as the psalmist continues, we hear this message loud and clear as he describes all the places where God is present, on the earth and beyond. First he declares that God is in the "heavens" and in "Sheol." In Hebrew cosmology, the heavens were conceived of as a vault above the earth—clearly separate from the earth and inaccessible by human beings. The heavens were the dwelling place of the transcendent God, so of course it is no surprise that the psalmist conceives of God as being in heaven. What is surprising is the psalmist's imagining of himself ascending to the heavens, where God is! This would have been a novel formulation at a time in Israel's history when there was no clearly developed idea of an afterlife in heaven with God.

In fact, any notion of an afterlife is found only in the shadowy existence of the dead in "Sheol." In Ancient Near Eastern thought, Sheol was the underworld, the abode of the dead, a dark and dusty place where the dead existed but did not

WATERS ABOVE FIRMAMENT
FIRMAMENT
windows (floodgates of heaven)
EARTH
mountains
mountains
sea
sea
Sheol (Hades)
Rahab
Leviathan
WATERS BENEATH EARTH

No one conceived of God as being present in Sheol! And indeed, it is sometimes hard for us to perceive God's presence in our darkest times and places. What does the psalmist want us to know, even when we feel alone, abandoned, or lifeless?

really *live*. In Sheol, which was thought to be in the depths of the earth (see, for example, Job 11:8), there were no relationships, no praise of God, no knowledge, and certainly no pleasure (see Psalms 6:6 and 88:4-13). As bold as his imagining himself in heaven is, the psalmist is now imagining that God is present even in this dark and dusty place of shadows! God's omnipresence is real, tangible, and absolutely pervasive. God is even in the places where we would never imagine him.

Another pair of opposites reiterates God's ever-presence: "If I take the wings of dawn and dwell beyond the sea." For the psalmist, the dawn (where the sun rises) symbolized the east, and the sea (the Mediterranean, west of Israel) signified the west. Up, down, east, west—wherever the psalmist can imagine himself, God is there.

Is there anywhere the psalmist can go to escape God? Apparently not! God is in the place of the living and the place of the dead; God is above the earth and deep within it; God is east

and God is west. Another anthropomorphic touch rounds out this section: "Even there your hand guides me, your right hand holds me fast."

The psalmist's description is so powerful that it may strike us that a God who is all-knowing and always-present might overwhelm us. God knows our words before we speak; God encircles us. But the tone of the psalm reassures us. This is not an overwhelming presence that controls us. Rather, it is a loving presence that knows us inside and out, with all of our strengths and all of our faults, a guiding presence that will never abandon us.

The psalms are full of declarations of praise and awe-filled musings about the incredible power of God. In this very special psalm we see that God's glory—his power and might—is defined not by the creation of the universe or the ability of God to defeat any enemy. Rather, God's glory is found in his intimacy with every human being, his very deliberate kinship with each one of us. The God who holds all things in existence and dwells on high is the same God whose hand guides us, whose right hand holds us fast. This is our God, who arrives in our lives continuously, whose enduring presence we celebrate during this Advent season.

One way God encounters us in the present is in sacraments. In fact, a simple definition of a sacrament is "an encounter with Christ." How have you encountered Jesus in the sacraments, especially in the Eucharist? Is there a verse from this psalm that helps you describe this divine encounter?

Praying the Word / Sacred Reading

Another excerpt from the second half of Psalm 139 offers us a remarkably personal prayer experience. In this section, the psalmist talks to God about his own formation in the womb. The overwhelming message is that God knew us before we were born. God created each of us, "knitting us" in the wombs of our mothers.

Before you say these words, close your eyes and imagine God as he imagined you. Imagine the delight he took in who you are. Imagine the miraculous creation of your mind, heart, and body in the womb of your mother. Thank God for the gift of your life and the love God showed you even before you were born.

¹³You formed my inmost being;
    you knit me in my mother's womb.
¹⁴I praise you, because I am wonderfully
    made;
    wonderful are your works!
    My very self you know.
¹⁵My bones are not hidden from you,
    When I was being made in secret,
    fashioned in the depths of the earth.
¹⁶Your eyes saw me unformed;
    in your book all are written down;
    my days were shaped, before one came
        to be. (Ps 139:13-16)

Living the Word

Our reflections have centered on a basic characteristic of meaningful relationships: presence. In Psalm 139, the psalmist is writing about his relationship with God. Our relationships with one another also require presence in order to be successful and life-giving.

What are some ways you can be more present to others this Advent? Is there anyone that you have neglected in any way—by not visiting or calling, or by simply not giving your full attention even when you are physically present? How can you be present to this person as God is present to you? Think of this as your own "advent" or "arrival" in this person's life in a new and committed way.

[handwritten notes in margins:] God's presence

Turning our mind to God thru out overday

Mindful awareness during everyday activities

right now the work of the moment is to become the person of Love

need to relize that every present moment is what we have to live in

Anticipating the Fullness of Encounter with Christ

Before prayerfully reading the following passage from the Second Letter of Peter, ask God to open your mind and heart.

2 Peter 3:3-4, 8-14

[3]Know this first of all, that in the last days scoffers will come [to] scoff, living according to their own desires [4]and saying, "Where is the promise of his coming? From the time when our ancestors fell asleep, everything has remained as it was from the beginning of creation." . . . [8]But do not ignore this one fact, beloved, that with the Lord one day is like a thousand years and a thousand years like one day. [9]The Lord does not delay his promise, as some regard "delay," but he is patient with you, not wishing that any should perish but that all should come to repentance. [10]But the day of the Lord will come like a thief, and then the heavens will pass away with a mighty roar and the elements will be dissolved by fire, and the earth and everything done on it will be found out. [11]Since

everything is to be dissolved in this way, what sort of persons ought [you] to be, conducting yourselves in holiness and devotion, [12]waiting for and hastening the coming of the day of God, because of which the heavens will be dissolved in flames and the elements melted by fire. [13]But according to his promise we await new heavens and a new earth in which righteousness dwells. [14]Therefore, beloved, since you await these things, be eager to be found without spot or blemish before him, at peace.

The information provided below in "Setting the Scene" will help you understand this passage's place in the New Testament and its relationship to the Advent season.

Setting the Scene

We have spent time reflecting on God's "arrivals" in the past and present. Now we will consider God's future arrival in the second coming of Jesus. Early Christians used the Greek word *parousia* when speaking of this highly anticipated event. *Parousia* literally means "presence" and was a term used in the Greco-Roman culture to describe the visit of an important dignitary or king. Of course, Jesus is the greatest "dignitary" of all, and his glorious return was expected to happen soon. According to Jesus and then his apostles, Jesus' *parousia* or *coming* would be a time of judgment but also a time of triumph and joy. The faithful believed they would be gathered up with Christ to share in the abundance of his everlasting kingdom (see, for example, 1 Thess 4:17).

The Second Letter of Peter is one of the latest books of the New Testament (if not the latest), likely written in the late first century or early second century. It reflects a time when the Christian community was grappling with the reality that Christ had not returned during the lifetimes of the first generation of Christians, including apostles such as Peter and Paul. The author of 2 Peter (likely a member of Peter's community writing after his death) is exhorting Christians to stay the course—Christ *will* return, and the faithful must always be prepared for his coming. The letter is intended to instill in its readers a renewed sense of faith in God's promises, hope in the second coming of Jesus, and the ultimate peace that comes from living in anticipation of final unity with Christ.

Note: Although the probable late date of composition makes it unlikely that 2 Peter was written by Peter himself, I will use the name "Peter" when speaking of the author for the sake of simplicity.

handwritten margin note: death should not cause people to grieve like unbelievers. there is a bright prospect of seeing departed believers again

*As you explore the passage from the Second Letter of Peter
in more detail, take note of the questions in the margin, using
them for group discussion or personal prayer and study.*

Understanding the Scene Itself

³**Know this first of all, that in the last days scoffers will come [to] scoff, living according to their own desires ⁴and saying, "Where is the promise of his coming? From the time when our ancestors fell asleep, everything has remained as it was from the beginning of creation."** . . .

The beginning of our passage is just as relevant today as it was two thousand years ago. At the end of the first century, opponents of Christianity and even false teachers within Christianity were ridiculing the apostolic teaching that Christ would return. Peter calls these folks "scoffers." In language reminiscent of Old Testament passages such as Psalm 42:11 ("Where is your God?"), the scoffers claim that Jesus has not kept his promise to return and that everything is the same as it always has been.

Peter indicates that this mocking attitude of the "scoffers" goes hand in hand with a sinful lifestyle, for they are "living according to their own desires" rather than living in expectation of God's judgment and presence. This idea will be developed further in the final section of our passage when Peter will clearly link faith in the *parousia* of Jesus with striving to live a holy life. The reference to our ancestors falling asleep is unclear. It may refer back to the great Israelites

As Christians, we believe that God has "arrived" in the world in a special way in the incarnation of Christ. But have things really changed because of this incarnate presence? Or has everything remained the same?

of the past such as Abraham and Moses. Or it may be a reference to the death of the apostles and the first generation of Christians. Regardless, the reference is intended to detract from the reality of Christ's return. It is as though the scoffers are saying, "If he hasn't come yet, he isn't coming."

The ongoing relevance of these claims is not lost on the modern reader. We have all heard the voice of such "scoffers," and indeed, sometimes that voice is inside our own minds and hearts. At times we may look at the hundreds of years that have passed since the promise of Jesus that he would return. We too may be tempted to say "everything has remained as it was from the beginning of creation"! And so the remainder of Peter's message will be of great value to us.

Finally, note that Peter says this scoffing is taking place "in the last days." It is clear that Christians at this time still believed that the return of Christ was imminent. They were living in "the last days" before this event would occur. This conviction is still very much a part of our Christian outlook. Christ has ushered in a new era, and regardless of how many actual days pass before his return, we are living in the final period of existence—the "last days" between the resurrection of Jesus and the resurrection of all the faithful at his coming.

The author of 2 Peter insists that even though God sometimes delays (from our perspective) in keeping his promises, this does not mean that he will not keep them. Has God ever seemed to "delay" in keeping promises to you? Did this experience lead you to doubt God or trust in God even more?

[8]But do not ignore this one fact, beloved, that with the Lord one day is like a thousand years and a thousand years like one day. [9]The Lord does not delay his promise, as some regard "delay," but he is patient with you, not wishing that any should perish but that all should come to repentance. [10]But the day of the Lord will come like a thief, and then the heavens will pass away with a mighty roar and the elements will be dissolved by fire, and the earth and everything done on it will be found out.

We receive eternal life with him

"time does not limit God" r God is outside of time.

Peter's creative turn of phrase that with God "one day is like a thousand years and a thousand years like one day" is an echo of Psalm 90:4, where the idea attested to the psalmist's wonder at God's eternity in comparison with the brevity of human life. Here Peter uses the phrase to explain a key concept to his audience: God's concept of time is not like ours. The one who lives in eternity does not mark time the way human beings do—day by day, month by month, year by year, century by century. Rather, God is beyond time. Logically then, what feels like "a long time" to us is not necessarily "a long time" by God's standards. We may think God is taking too long to keep his promises. God does not necessarily agree.

Peter then explains the delay in Christ's coming

another way. God's seeming delay is not because he does not care. Rather, God delays *because he is patient*. God wants to give human beings every opportunity to repent so that no one will "perish." Thus Peter has placed an important theme of Scripture (God's desire that all be saved; e.g., 1 Tim 2:4) in the context of the timetable of Jesus' return: God intentionally delays the return of Christ so that more people have time to repent and be saved. *wow*

However, this benevolent delay should not be taken as a sign that we can become lax and unprepared. Peter reminds us that the day of the Lord "will come like a thief" (echoing the words of Jesus himself in passages such as Matt 24:43). At this time, there will be a great change. The heavens (the cosmos) and the earth as we know them will "pass away," making way for the newness of God's kingdom.

Peter describes God as patient. We might recall God's description of himself to Moses: "the LORD, the LORD, a God gracious and merciful, slow to anger and abounding in love and fidelity" (Exod 34:6). In what ways has God been patient with you? Is God being patient with the whole human race?

Why do you think Jesus said that he would return "like a thief" in the night (see Matt 24:43; 1 Thess 5:2; Rev 3:3)? Do you find this language frightening or inspiring?

11Since everything is to be dissolved in this way, what sort of persons ought [you] to be, conducting yourselves in holiness and devotion, **12**waiting for and hastening the coming of the day of God, because of which the heavens will be dissolved in flames and the elements melted by fire. **13**But according to his promise we await new heavens and a new earth in which righteousness dwells.

Verses 10-13 incorporate typical eschatological language (or language used to describe the end time) to describe the future "day of the Lord." This day of the Lord (or "day of God" as it is called here) was expected to be a day of

God isn't patient b/c we deserve it. He's patient b/c it's who he is.

He doesn't love patience w/ those loves since patience is his very n

divine intervention and judgment, the day God would finally come to vanquish all of his enemies, renew the earth, and invite the faithful ones to join in his triumph. Although the end result of this day of the Lord was joyous for God's people, the process was often described in the Old Testament in frightening terms of human fear and cosmic destruction (see, for example, Isa 13). The end result of this eschatological upheaval is the renewal of the faithful and their home with God—new heavens and a new earth.

The heart of Peter's message is found in this section as he tries to convince Christians that there is an inherent relationship between *expectation of the future return of Jesus* and *the way we live our lives right now*. If we believe that the day of the Lord is coming—that Jesus will come in power and glory to judge his people and invite the faithful ones to be with him forever—then we must live in constant expectation of this day. How do we do this? According to Peter, we wait for Christ by "conducting [ourselves] in holiness and devotion."

> The second coming of Jesus is often described in Scripture in symbolic imagery that can be quite alarming (fire, destruction, battles, etc.). Of course, no one knows exactly what this "arrival" will look like or be like. How do you envision the Parousia of Christ? What words would you use to describe this awesome reality?

Just like our remembering of God's past "arrivals," our waiting for God's future "arrival" is meant to be an active experience, not a passive one. We do not just sit around waiting for Jesus to return. We do not live however we would like until he comes, thinking he does not care what we do or uncertain whether he will return at all. Rather, we are to conduct ourselves in holiness and devotion. We are to live in such a way that our lives reflect the holiness of God and demonstrate our faithfulness toward God and his people.

In this way, Peter quite remarkably claims that we not only *wait for* but actually *hasten* the return of Christ! It seems very bold indeed to claim that human beings can influence the timing of the day of the Lord, and yet, if Peter's claim is that God delays Jesus' return in order to allow us to repent, then this is a logical conclusion. If we do repent and live accordingly, then there is no longer reason to delay!

[14]**Therefore, beloved, since you await these things, be eager to be found without spot or blemish before him, at peace.**

We can read this final admonition as words spoken directly to us in our time of Advent longing. Using the intimate term "beloved" as he has throughout this passage, Peter encourages us in our waiting to be "eager" to live spotless lives. Now, of course, it is impossible to never sin, to never miss the mark or fail in the love to which we are called. But our eagerness to meet Jesus when he arrives will be a constant source of inspiration as we strive to live according to his will. If we do this, we will have peace.

The biblical notion of "holiness" is not just keeping out of trouble or praying a lot. To be holy is to be sacred—set apart, different, special. How should Christians set themselves apart? How are we "other" than the scoffers mentioned in verses 3-4? How are we to live in a way that is demonstrably different than that of the world, as we wait in eager expectation of the coming of Jesus?

spotless (line)

How do your encounters with Christ in the Eucharist help you to both experience his presence and long for his presence? How would you explain this spiritual mystery to others?

The strands of our Advent longing and our sense of God's "arrivals" in the past, present, and future have come together in one name, one Person: Jesus Christ. It is Christ who is the Word made flesh dwelling among us. It is Christ who is the constant presence from which we cannot and will not flee. It is Christ who will arrive again in the fullness of time to encounter us in peace. As we wait and as we long, may we join together in the hopeful prayer of every Christian: *Come, Lord Jesus!*

In the Eucharist God shows his Love for us the Eucharist sustains the life of the soul. gives us grace we need

Come, Lord Jesus!

you experience peace and joy when you receive Jesus

Praying the Word / Sacred Reading

Jesus was known to tell his followers to be watchful and alert as they lived in expectation of his return (e.g., Mark 13:33). Reflect on the following words of Christ:

"May he not come suddenly and find you sleeping. What I say to you, I say to all: 'Watch!'" (Mark 13:36-37)

Pray with the following questions:

What is "sleepiness" in your own life, and how can you guard against it?

What is "watchfulness," and how is it the proper attitude of the loving, faithful, and hopeful Christian? How do you keep watch?

Do you conceive of Advent as a special time to keep watch for the coming of Christ in your life right now and at the end of the age?

Now talk to Jesus in your own words, asking him to help you to be watchful and to ward off sleepiness. Pray that your Advent may be a special time of watchfulness as you prepare your heart for his coming. End your prayer with the final prayer of Scripture: "Come, Lord Jesus!" (Rev 22:20)

Living the Word

The Second Letter of Peter is presented as a final exhortation of the apostle Peter, who senses that his death is near. In 1:13-15, he writes: "I think it right, as long as I am in this 'tent,' to stir you up by a reminder, since I know that I will soon have to put it aside, as indeed our Lord Jesus Christ has shown me. I shall also make every effort to enable you always to remember these things after my departure."

Peter's desire to "stir up" his community with his teaching, which he desires to pass along as a firm belief, is a powerful part of the vitality of the Christian community, which exists to this

Handwritten margin notes:
Meaning
Not
being
fruitful

esp.
Jesus in advent
is saying
"wake up, listen
watch

FYI the
devil prowls
around
seeking whom
he might devour

THANKFUL
• for God's
sacrifice,
grace,
mercy,
& blessing

day because of the passing on of beliefs from one generation to the next, from one community to the next, from one person to another.

Reflect for a time on your own experience of this "stirring up" in faith that has allowed you to "remember these things" as part of the Christian community:

Who shared with you the gift of faith while living in this "tent" of earthly existence?

Who are you called to "stir up" in faith during your own life?

How is this dynamic of sharing faith a way that God continues to "arrive" in this world until the second coming of Christ?

How can you take a more active role in proclaiming Christ as you await the day of the Lord?

engage in disciple

Show God's love
by Listening
w/Generosity
by Encouraging
@

be patient
Humili
obedience